At
the Foot
of the Mountain

TAK Erzinger

D1564974

Floricanto Press

Floricanto is a trademark of *Floricanto Press*.

Berkeley Press is an imprint of Inter-American Development, Inc.

Floricanto Press

7177 Walnut Canyon Rd.

Moorpark, California 93021

(415) 793-2662

www.floricantoPress.com

ISBN: 978-1-951088-25-5

Library of Congress Control Number: 2021932454

"Por nuestra cultura hablarán nuestros libros. Our books shall speak for our culture."

Roberto Cabello-Argandoña, Editor

Reviews of *At the Foot of the Mountain*

In *At the Foot of the Mountain*, TAK Erzinger creates a poetic landscape of delightful solitude. Nature becomes much more than a mere surrounding or backdrop in Erzinger's poems; it is a companion, a remedy, a living, breathing part of the poet's being. Erzinger's brave poetic voice seeks strength in fragility and wholeness in the fragmented, allowing us to immerse ourselves in the delicately moving truth of her poetry. —**Andriana Minou, Poet, writer and Judge Eyeland Book Awards**

TAK Erzinger is one of my favourite writers. Her words work beautifully on the page and as audio fiction. It has been a pleasure to work with her in producing her work for our podcast. She has a magical-realist vision that is both surprising and familiar to those who enjoy that genre and this is evident in both her poetry and prose. As befits an accomplished artist, her words have colour and richness that reward repeated reading and savouring of each line. —**Christopher Gregory, Producer and Director, *Alt.Stories* and *Fake Realties Podcasts***

At the Foot of the Mountain sees TAK Erzinger evolving further as a master of style and sentiment. There is a vividness, depth, and accessibility to these poems that make them easily digestible yet profoundly enduring. Whether literal or metaphorical, personal or universal, Erzinger's work will resonate with every reader. —**Jordan Blum, Founder, Editor-in-Chief, *The Bookends Review***

At the Foot of the Mountain showcases the remarkable talent of TAK Erzinger. Each poem in the collection is exceptional. The poems are a haunting exploration of the human soul. Drawing on Erzinger's own experiences and her clear love of nature, these are poems you will want to read again and again. My personal favourite is Chemical Bonds, a poem that is so perfectly beautiful and tragic that I want to share it with everyone I know. **—Sheila Bugler, Author** *Before You Were Gone*

At
the Foot
of the Mountain

Acknowledgments

Many thanks to the editors of the following magazines, journals and reviews, in which some of the poems have previously appeared.

The Avocet Journal: "Red Kite" 2nd publication "Sacrilege" "Testament"
The Beautiful Space Journal: "Boundary Survey" "Wanderweg" "The Landing"
Bien Acompañada, Cornell University "The Food's Delicious, You're Not Welcome" "Salsa Fresca"
The Cirrus Poetry Review: "Phantom Pains"
Grey Borders Magazine: "Deer at the Border" "Migratory Patterns"
Harness Magazine: "Latin Roots" "Threadbare"
The Feminine Collective: "Ménage à trois"
The Journal of Wild Culture: "At the Foot of the Mountain" "Holy" "Reflection"
Lust for Life Journal: 2nd publication "Boundary Survey"
Mojave He[art] Review: "Chemical Bonds" "The Contrition Between Us"
The Opiate Magazine: "Orphan"
A New Ulster: "Clothe Me" "Irreplaceable Code" "Reflection" (2nd publishing) "Sol" (2nd publishing)
Quince Magazine: "Body"
The Rising Phoenix Review: "Sacrilege" "Sans Frontières"
South River Poetry Wilkes University: "Fallen"
Vita Brevis Press: "Sol"
Woolf Journal of Literature and Culture: "Afternoon Route" "Denouement" "Overtime"

Dedicated to all those who have been suffering in silence, may you find the strength to get the support you need and finally be able to step outside.

§ § §

"Someone I loved once gave me a box full of darkness. It took me years to understand that this too, was a gift." — **Mary Oliver**

TABLE OF CONTENTS

Clothe Me

Clothe me, all those lost things-
cuckoo eggs left in
spring nests,
homeless migrating hopes and dreams
fish attempting to eat
indigestible things
Clothe me, all those lost things-
lips cracked from silence
time crashing in like a storm on a shore
disposable hours, disposable things,
disposable nature, disposable truths
don't leave me
don't leave me
don't leave me:
it has escaped like a bird from a cage,
free or hunted
but without remorse.

Phantom Pains

Ghosts
I open my eyes
morning yawns.

At the bedside
whispers cling, strings
of beads on empty webs.

I listen
liquid light, leaks
through the windows.

"Wake up child"
Mountains of chest, falling
a landscape of memories.

I sit and wait to rise
as the voices
fade.

From Behind the Window

The lady's stereo played a jazz song,
it was blue.
The lady was painting,
the paint was blue.
The lady's fingers smudged the painting,
they turned blue.
They lady's eyes filled with tears,
they were blue.
The autumn sky outside the window,
it was blue.
The delphiniums leaning against the sky,
they were almost blue.
The lady opened the window to clear her head
and cut her hand.
Her hand turned red.
She saw the geraniums on the window sill, they were red.
Blood spilled from her hand onto the paper
blotting the blue paint red, like the flowers on her sill.
She bandaged her hand and dried her eyes.

The lady stepped outside
sunshine washed across her cheeks,
they became red.
Everything coloured,
like a new palette and she felt a pull,
drawing her
one step further away
from her monochromatic memories.

Hidden in Plain Sight

Peace
has been forgotten lately
so she's retreated. She hides
behind the curtains, alone in the
dark like a burrowed mole.
She keeps hoping her absence
will be noticed.

She knows she's a lot of work
but she wants you to know
with a little nurturing
her rewards are priceless.

Red Kite

You follow me
as I walk past the field of wheat
near the lake.

You glide above me,
as if to cast a shadow on my sorrow.

The pace and my movement,
seem to conform to your flight,
I think.

Landing on a fence post
you wait, your smoothed down feathers,
glistening in liquid light,
head cocked with interest.

In the morning, when I enter my garden,
I can hear you, keeping watch above the
poppies and cornflowers,
outside, no boundaries, inside nature.

The currents carry your call,
window to window, so many
heated afternoons, ignored
by most.

I hear you hunting.

As the season turns, I have noticed
your absence.

Maybe you've flown
over to the valley, south east,
where you've gone to roost,
massive kites,
against a forget-me-not sky.

I keep awaiting your return.

Totem

Hawks

        above
             and
                 below
the clouds.

Are they aware,
            their shadows
tattoo
            the landscape's
round belly

     road maps

courtesy of
       the sun?

Do they know
    the power

of their

        presence,

guiding souls

        who

        beg to discover

the contours

        their path?

Overtime

Tireless
bees swim against the wind's tide
working overtime

flowers oblige
extending their opening hours

and still leaves fall like stars
a colouring of comets

they drift to unknown spaces
unconcerned by their fate

letting go.

Unlike us.

Exhausted
we cling to broken branches
beyond repair.

Unabashed

Creek bed: clear green
washes all stones
un-rough in smooth grip

when the light
spills and it is

mid-week, no one is aware
skins shed. Trees strip
slipping off garments
well-worn, hampers piled high
fallen secrets left

unhidden. The afternoon
appears in front
of a hallow sky.
I follow the trail and cross

the fresh and fragile fungi,
which want to compete with
the trees.

Our harvest sun
more like a god
cupped in cosmos.

Trains and an impatient phone, fast,
hum, unrelenting. And buzzard call

all drowned out in the rush
of an endless waterfall.

Serenade

In that cradle of trees, leaves,
were sienna, golden, alight.

I witnessed the wind, how
softly it would rock the branches,

lullabies, from afar. The stream was
an eager audience in cleft earth,

its appraisal I longed to match.
Without judgement, without concern

without fear of flooding over.
I listened for a music I could

understand, like lyrics
the forest offered a chorus

of hidden wildlife, the mountain's back
supporting them, loud enough to hear

not see. I tried to match the tone
but my voice froze each time

my mouth opened. I listened for
words I could catch, so many

falling leaves, heard the branches
drop their notes. In that cradle of

trees, I discovered I was part
of that rhythm, this piece was

composed long ago. I paused
and hoped to be baptised

for the trees to lift me up and
swaddle me in song,

then bring the evening home
letting the low stars dance with me.

Chemical Bonds

Where have they
arrived from,
those tiny snowflakes
drifting in the early morning light
sprinkled from the heavens,
clinging for survival,
here and there,
on the lips of quivering petals
still pursing towards the sun?

What happened to that girl
the one they left behind,
captured like a snapshot
standing in the surf
at the edge of the shore,
now overrun with tourists,
the one who could never
find a shell?

Testament

Silently
snow huddles
on the lap of the hill;
flakes camouflaged.

Winter   midday
sunshine skates,   cuts
a smooth diamond on
a frozen sky.

Gossipy crows
chatter into the trees,
branches nod at whispers
from the wind.

Everything frozen
in ice, a yellow birch leaf
entombed
a testament
to a season once lived.

Latin Roots

The first foreign language
I ever heard, gave me a heat rush,
humid and wet. It sent back echoes of
ancestral cries, *una lengua* licking

around my ears. It hung in the air,
a concoction of intoxicating sounds
bouncing between the four walls of our
cramped kitchen. A salacious mix of

garlic, cumino, cilantro and lust.
Each word boiling over into a
simmering, sexy recipe that has
been cultivated and passed down

from the sweltering Amazon.
Its *vulgar* origins rolling over a vast
ocean from the Iberian-peninsula,
delivering an unwanted and twisted package.

Its contents bastardized the native balance
and shackled those mysterious beings
from the heart of a dark continent,
creating a language developed from pain.

Through this unwanted merger
sweaty bongo beats and rapid rhythms,
played out into a dialect of stolen heritages
communicating in a devilish dance of

wagging tongue and swinging hips.
I heard it first from my mother, it reverberated
through her, between the four walls of our
cramped kitchen. Her words poured forth

accentuated, pulsated and thick.
I listened as the exposure of a hidden
history came rolling out in sensual sounds,
each syllable doing a salsa off her tongue,

teaching me the vernacular of our Latin roots.

The Missing Link

Genes aren't substituted. Sugar is substituted,
and its traces linger on wanting lips. Meat is substituted.
Hunger substituted by strangers—
the satiation of their substitution,
and its false sense of fullness,
can leave you starved. What is substituted is something
being replaced, something needing
to be filled, *to top off that glass*—
an action that says *there's no need to be empty.* The
skin and its landscape chart an area that genes
have formed, genes demarcate neither a home nor
a guarantee of love—
genes are a road map, a link, navigating
the distance from where we once began.

Orphan

When your mother decides to leave,
do you tell the world?

What if everyone thinks it's your fault?

You could pretend it didn't happen,
never talk about it and over-compensate with many things,
become an awesome painter
share your artwork full of hidden meaning.

Maybe people will forget to ask.

It will push you to develop in ways you never imagined,
maybe ways she would've been proud of, if she'd been
around.

Like how you can really dance, the way she could always dance, the way you followed her steps to the beats of all the albums she bought you,
holding hands, she'd swing you around and around, pulling you close and pushing you back,
keeping you spinning,
you'd hear, *I'll always be there for you.*

It's not what she said though.

She was only singing.

Madre

Madre, your language is full of exotic sounds
With each sound you produce, I hear something else.
I am a part of you, and part
Of a place you'll never be able to pronounce. In the kitchen
When you've shared that space with me,
Recipes are revealed like unsent letters from the past,
I ask, how, do you separate the plantain from its husk—
Have I missed something in translation?
Although it's clear to you. But still I need to know
The secret behind the preparation, how you peeled it all
away. "Well," you tell me, "swiftly, not to bruise the fruit."
Tender, I stand next to you, unable to comprehend your
actions.

Off Road

I've searched for you in wrinkled recipes
filling up on silence, words a meal will never convey. I've
searched for you in the waking hours, hoarding pockets of
sunshine, the kind that never burns.
I've searched for you in the constellations of freckles,
moles and scars, the galaxy that stretches across my skin.
I've searched for you in the tangle of my hair, its density
like the Amazon, a place you might have touched.
I've searched for you in accents, the ones that are rich
and thick.
I've searched for you blindly,   a bat,
chasing the echoes of the past.

What would it mean to find you?

What would it mean
to stop searching
for a person
who
never bothered
to notice
I was missing?

Boundary Survey

The psychologists have been told to survey my psyche.
They're trying to see if my mind is a mountain range

full of jagged precipices or a desert, bare boned and dry.
They begin topographically, looking at the contours of my
landscape,

the existing features, the surface of my earth.
They need to scale its territory to see if it's flat like the

soles of my shoe or round like a helium balloon straining
to escape behind the clouds. They've been ordered to map
out the places

unknown. They want to know if the visible network of
roads leads to the eye of the storm, is there still a buildable
base there?

There is a place they will never be able to access.
At night, the sweat hangs around my forehead, a crown of pearls,

my eyes are wide shut and filled with sand and I become your princess again. I meet you there at the surf's edge.

We chase crabs on the beach and you teach me about the stars. The only bottles in sight are the ones filled with messages

we launch into the ocean. In the morning, I taste the salt on my cheeks and they'll think it's from tears.

They'll never be able to reach the outer banks of that place. I don't want it to go into their draft.

Certain terrains are required to be left alone.

Denouement[1]

In the opening act of the year, the hills
are ivory white, unfurled, fresh.

I watch the crows, in a row
piano keys, playing to an invisible metronome,

their tempo, in time, a serenade
coaxing at the drama percolating

under the soil. The sun draws closer,
taking centre stage,   teasing

causing the landscape to sweat in anticipation,
freckling in dots of green, little tips

---

1   *The final part of a play in which the strands of the plot are drawn together and matters are explained or resolved;* The outcome of a situation, when something is decided or made clear.

alien fingers reaching out, revealing a preview
of the next scene about to begin

like an audience member, I am transfixed

as the coming season slowly makes
her entrance.

Rambler's Road

Like Dorothy in those red shoes,
she found herself lost between

all that had been written and all
that was speculation.

The path curled its index finger
beckoning her to follow.

Its great spine stretched out
giving her support, an entrance

into the belly of the forest
aching to be heard

hungry for peace
from the chatter

of the unnatural world.

Wanderweg

A call to the trail, away from the trajectory of a therapist's chair.
An awakening. Slivers of sunlight peek into an unfinished dream.

A call to the living, "Step outside!"

A crash to the bottom now requires a slow crawl back to the top,
a task set at hand, to get moving, start walking.

A call to the wild.

To wander within it with hopes of wandering away from an invisible illness that's screaming to escape.

Standing alone above the horizon, patchwork hills roll into mismatched greens opening my heart to change.

An invitation from the wind, a call to post-illness instead of post-traumatic, a welcome to post-despair from a friendly sky.

It embraces me like a plush pullover its sunbeams fall
upon my cheeks like golden fingers and dry away my tears.

A march towards a path reaching out to me through
generations,
worn down by those seeking penance.

Contrition. Walking into the woods, up through the hills
around the mountains, above the lakes, through the sleepy
villages

in hopes of shedding this second skin of singular sadness.

Not   a   choice,   but   a   scar.

As I pass the lake's edge I imagine I'm the water
supporting the sailboats, the burden placed upon my back
and

the buoyancy of those troubles forced up again and again,
like the force
keeping the boats afloat, normalcy slipping between my
fingertips.

Yet, here I am amid the trees, marching upon the path to recovery, learning to let go, to just be in that moment in time,

embracing forgiveness between the rustle of the leaves and the march of my feet.

Secondary Growth*

What is it that
keeps some standing,
those lanky branches
twisting in the wind,
shaken leaves refusing
to let go, clinging to limbs
steadfast and solid,
as the storm rages
from all sides,
whipping and howling
from its eye?

*In botany, secondary growth is a result from
cell division that causes the stem and the roots to thicken

What becomes of
the child that once was,
caught between the turmoil
the four walls of that home
revisited in dreams,
molecular traces left
on seams of their skin,
now empty arms,
the way she often
bent backwards and buckled
to keep the calm?

The Landing

When they tell you, you've
had a nervous breakdown
you become like an astronaut

you find yourself drifting,
pleading for someone to provide you
with the right equipment.

In the right space
you can deploy like the Eagle
confronting the "magnificent desolation" resolutely.

To be able to sink your feet into the
lunatic surface will be a revelation
tip-toeing through craters formed

long before you were born.
If you run low on fuel
at least you will have finally seen

what those wounds look like
up close and personal and like
the dark side of the moon

allow the parts unseen to be
tucked back into the envelope
of your universe.

The discovery-
every exploration takes time
and patience.

Ménage à trois

My features, they betray me
with their inside joke,
my identity comprised of an awkward three-some.

But when I'm drunk, so I've heard,
the southern drawl spills
out like molasses.

I've lived my life as a chameleon,
camouflaging into the background,
hidden in someone else's wild.

I shake my hips to any salsa beat
and can't speak without using my hands
my Latin refuses to be evicted.

Your heritage houses your soul.

But here in the valley, I've drawn
curtains around my heart,
making sure to keep its volume down.
Blending in like the furniture.

Still not quite enough, but almost tolerable
and yet my walk, that Yankee doodle gait,
gives my secret away and I cannot deny
my body the satisfaction

of its original sin.

The Afternoon Route

Lost in the Alp's crooked smile
a toothpick between those Myths, there
I stood a cowgirl without boots
from America to Heidiland
fleeing ghosts who knew no boundaries.

I hiked up the pilgrim's way and slipped
down behind the trees
I find myself at middle age
in the afternoon, following a map
to unknown places.

Fallen in the mountain's crevasse,
I fell from who I was,
with my rucksack full of southern charm
tucked in like a snail
fearful of being exposed

but I find Tell at the apple orchard
and create my own rebellion
guided by the country light
I follow to catch Victoria's view
and mourn like she did there for Albert.

Dusk. I watch bats
chase away the day.

The sky is busy. Stars
are preparing for their entrance.

A distant chapel chimes.
Cows are called home
and pastures are left open.

Within a rolling valley
I end up rooted like a perennial
anchored firmly in the soil.

Canto de mi Sangre | Song of my Blood

The day my Caribbean aunt
heavily accented
peered at me and said

you're not Latina,
did I boil like *arroz*
or salted *yucca*, tough to resist?

A lifetime, I've paraded you-
your pulse, pumping beneath my olive skin,
revealing everything.

I've been told you're too high,
beta blockers to slow the flow
steal the rhythm of my step

see, the sun is red,
the streets are white and the veins blue
in other words, *you were born here*

and you're different than us,
I swallow this large pill
diluting what flows through me.

Wash away my aunt's words
who only cooks Colombian food
high in fat and carbs,

I eat it up hungrily,
attempting to digest enough
to return to my natural state.

Sol

Oftentimes the sun freshly awoken hangs
as if a ripe fruit, like it's an orange-
or maybe a gold coin unearthed; egg yolk spilt
between cracked peaks. It rolls out this morning
glowing on the valley, past the emerging hills
where I tread by bare trees, recalling matchsticks.
Vertebrae aligned with smooth stones,
bearing each step, then disappearing in leaves.

It's there, I recognise that I'm alight, am ready to burst,
the matured fruit. It's me who has arisen, deciding to follow
the country road, up early, sliding the hill down,
illuminating, I find that child dancing across the cackling
creek the brightest light: now loved, now free.

Reflection

What lies we see   What, be?
Based on public image   imagine
Stories filtered   fake
Cropping out sorrow,   happiness
If we could return to our origins.   forgotten.
What makes us human?   Conscience,
What if we could access that place   outside
together?   ourselves

Unafraid of deeper instincts   wild,
Embracing our Earth's   nature
call for help,   healing
finally living in truth.   in peace.

Threadbare

The colours we've worn are fading.
They've been bleached by the sun,
left on the clothesline too long.
Materials amassed by the hands of hope
washed ashore like faceless pebbles
looking for a land to smooth away the rougher edges,
a place to settle in the earth.

Those colours, threads connecting people
woven into a textile of language, culture and heritage.
Colours refracted, like a prism, caught between
barstools, classrooms, offices and kitchen tables
creating a rainbow, the kind we've always wished upon.
A fanned out tapestry stitched together by our ancestors,
who toiled with their mismatched yarn to create this life.

With scissor tongues sharpened by fear
the very fabric of what has held us together
is being cut apart, left in shreds like a tattered
flag helpless against the wind. The ideals that
clothed us, hang off us now, we stand awkwardly
like children playing dress-up in something
that doesn't look or feel quite right.

To go outside, we find it again, nature's palette
before our eyes, bright and diverse the way it was
intended to be. A migration of birds skein
across the sky reminding us of the spots that need to
be repaired. The first gaping hole needs a darning.

Who will pick up the stitch, knitting up the wound,
before we become completely unravelled?

Sans Frontières

They are little birds of prey
fleeing the nest too early.

Confused, their flight is crooked
like the cage they just escaped from.

The moon, helpless, hides behind
a veil of sky, where stars stare in disbelief,

waiting for good-byes that are never spoken
for fear of the awakening sun.

Their flight forms a mosaic pattern of
mismatched colours, bleeding together

like gouache that is over saturated by water.
Their image threatened to be washed away.

Little tired wings, flutter, torn and bent, drift
over unsteady waves that hunger for their souls.

Neptune hears their cry and scolds the gluttonous sea.
He wants to save them and he offers them atonement.

He strips them of their tired feathers
replacing them with fins, calling to those children,

"Now you are able to swim." Their empty shells
left a drift, like snake skins on the sand

and off they dive mermaids, unbridled by any land.

Salsa Fresca

Tell me what's the flavour,
They'll say it's a fruit not a veg.

The squeeze, the slice, against the counter
hard top, spread open

spilt, drips its seeds
body to board. Decisions deliberate

mixing up the labour of ancient
gods, claiming stolen treasure

sun-kissed flesh dressed in
cumino, strong, in reprisal;

a dash of salt sprinkled
curing what was bruised,

stripped and diced cilantro
lands like gulls on a sea of red

swilled in lime and brimming in garlic.
Chips cut its surface

like those galleons piled high,
delivering a forgotten taste

of famine and plenty, spiced with
cultural appropriation in every bite.

The Food's Delicious, You're Not Welcome

Once adults become a certain age
it's a matter of time before they reminisce
to talk of the past
and say it was better

Ethnic food piled high
they'll question *Why, dear friend,*
aren't you afraid?
and lick their lips in satisfaction

It requires a stranger, light-skinned
without a funny surname
to offer up dishes, exotic recipes
on familiar ground

This individual, welcomed like a pet
loves the taste of cheeseburgers
heats up the grill
to fire up their lies

The irony of being accepted
the memory of a childhood
chewing her up and spitting her out
just a little taste

garlic sautéed softens
too much spice can ruin the meal
adulting in measured cups
does not guarantee the right flavour

The common denominator loves the food
but does that mean its balanced?
I've learnt to share those dishes while I continue
to get burned in places unseen and am
left with scorched pans, unable to replace them.

Migratory Patterns

How on earth do
they remember,
those arteries of rivers
pumping through the landscape,
regurgitated from oceans'
mouths, traveling from abroad
to and fro,
like flower seeds
ascending and dispersing
in the sky?

What happens now
to the children who fled,
their image captured in
a dated newspaper, drifting
on the water's edge
sidled by the heavens,
now consumed by gulls,
where good-byes were
never spoken for
fear of being lost?

Holy

When we step outside together
congregations of bees

kneel on the heads of daisies
their prayers deafening
if only we could give thanks so freely

never mind that our practice
differs; in the sunlight, our sins
tears of sweat, wiped away.

We pause, baptised by sky,
our fingers, rooted in one another's
trees branches rise extoling hallelujah!

Fallen

Trees found
suddenly naked

stripped

whistled by wind,
swaying, they bare it all

like skinned bones
utterly devoid of shame.

From the mouth
of the sky snow

tumbles down
season's whispers

revelations arriving
late like a bride

to a wedding
or a long-held secret.

And from the tail
of the trail

the moon bathes
those bare bodies

trees found
suddenly naked

stripped
baptised by light

washed clean.

Pneuma[2]

Then
the sky was easy to imbibe…
a sip now

another later…
a big swallow
always enough

inhaling the air
was a given
swilling clouds

around an eager tongue
down the throat
filled with guile

---

2 *Ancient Greek for breath, air; in a religious context "spirit or "soul"*

as if an endless reservoir
a communal place
suddenly polluted

taking for granted
that which was never seen.

The Relationship

We cling to you for shelter
and like a greedy lover, we
often ignore your needs,
asking for more than we deserve

taking for granted the abundance
of your beauty and love
secretly hoping you will not
notice, the abuse that we heap

upon you in our day-to-day lives.
We dread the day when
you've had enough because
without you,

we will be unable to survive.

Deprived [3]

No one's told them their time is up,
that their execution has been set.

There is no arraignment here,
the date has been planned without notice.

Innocently they welcome the day in their furry green attire.
They lean their proud heads against a forget-me-not sky,

swaying along to the bird songs, those gentle psalms
offered up daily in thanks and gratitude.

They are an alignment of protective mothers
housing an assortment of life, a temple of nests.

Like most mothers they have been taken for granted.
Their branches are strong arms that have weathered

---

3   *inspired after a group of spruce was felled near my home*

many a storm offering consoling embraces to
all those families in need of shelter and want.

They were the welcoming committee when I arrived
in this strange land, when words were nothing

but an assault of uncomfortable sounds,
attacking my ears and confusing my mind.

They consoled me during my loneliest hours,
when the sky clothed the evening in a petticoat of stars,

I leaned in close, as they whispered in
a rush of bat wings and rustling prayers.

In an instant those pillars of life will be
struck down, eaten alive by hungry jaws,

a whole habitat will be left homeless
without a chance to say good-bye

leaving me, and a generation orphaned.

Deer at the Border

Following the border of trees. Quietly.
Me, on the path, worried and anxious. Searching.
Beside me the whole time. Neither curious or
afraid, unlike me. Nothing spiritual, as some

would describe this creature, only a deer.
What about a deer? Out of a hunter's range.
A graceful deer. Peaceful vigilance.
The sun was just rising. Wind rustling the leaves.

What is it? A creature unto itself, natural.
Bow, bow, bowing its head. As innocent as you, forgiving
of what it doesn't know, taking only what it needs.
A gentle companion, false security by my side.

The forest a bastion, a busy old forest, working tirelessly?
We aren't even aware of it, but the deer is.

Migration

Ancient dust
bones of pharaohs
weathering forgotten histories

shattered giants
wafted sand
eager to take flight abroad

billowed dunes
storm-stir present
past civilisations unearthed

nomad winds exhaled
migrant-hasty
weightless grains arrive

sun-drenched glaciers
exposed await
nestled against the sky.

Sacrilege

It was a somber funeral
a graveyard for trees

with branches charred
like burnt chicken bones.

In the sunlight, we observed
those crooked fingers scratching

at the sky's blue skin as
lingering clouds of smoke

lifted like souls from lifeless bodies
not quite ready to be released.

Their sacred gathering had
been defiled by a blasphemer,

a non-believer in their truth
and they were set a light

and burnt like heretics with little
time for their congregation to

save their lives. We returned to
mourn, discovering our own

fragility, wagging its finger
at us in culpability, while the sea

nodded its head in hopeless prayer.

Waterfall

You are free
but cannot run past stones,

they divide you
splitting you apart.

Your body is fluid.
to keep you going, it flows creating ripples.

You open your mouth
and people fail to hear you are a waterfall.

You roll through the landscape
spilling past their feet where they

only know the buzz of their devices
but in your depth their haze is just clouds.

Your currents adhere to the weather
and it is clear, your stream cuts deep,

never stopping
you are always awake.

They cannot hold you still
your emotions topple from

the lip of the ledge forming words
leaving imprints on the body of this land.

Body

The house
of an object.

Its husk
or shell.

The dwelling,
the residence,

demarcation
lines.

The bottom
of forest's

floor and
tops of

trees.
An enclosure

or a box,
a cell,

a vessel.
And then:

the bright
open

windows
where

the light
of life

escapes.
That quick

spark of something
the threshold

point
that keeps

us one
and whole

a shelter
from where

we'll
go.

Crossing Over like a Lion's Tooth[4]

Dispersed
her ragged breath parachuted
like a *pappus*
dragging along the afternoon
of that spring day

she disappeared before our
eyes, like
landscape eaten up
by the fog
only her molecules remained,
staining every corner of our lives.

Is she kept aloft in a vortex
now, drifting across
the planet or the universe
floating aimlessly?

---

4   a dandelion

72

If only we were astronomers
we could chart her voyage
keeping a watchful eye
ensuring that the horizontal winds
delivered her safely to the stars.

The Contrition Between Us

We are like two cats circling,
insecure, heated, fearful.

Each one vying for his place,
seeds that have scattered haphazardly

breaking cracks in the cement,
vulnerable and strong at the same time.

It's like we've forgotten what brought
us to this place: the promises,

like a wide and clear spring sky, its
passing clouds, whispers tucked under

our pillows. The scent of love lingers,
over empty plates and glasses, still warm

from the summer's evening sun
easing the tension, making us forget

a moment about the family we will never
have.

Constellation of a Cottage Garden

There's the garden the toiled soil the wet of grass
                    and the rose bed

        uprooted

now

there's where hopes of children were buried
            and there's

                where we mourned

    and the perennials return

                reaching
        for
        light

and the vegetable patch
                and the stories sowed by our hands

at the table
    we eat our history

  there's something gained

buds full and heavy   burst

         between

        weeds run amok
     completing what we started

opening their mouths and   swallowing up bees

  the season's end   as we depart

  we've left scattered blueprints of an unfinished
thing—

unable to witness its end
         just like with some seeds or   stars.

The Conservation of Energy

Clearly it is day
above the mega-watt bulb with its
tentacles every which way
soundless.

Pulling at this, pulling at that.
I see it all around
I keep going.
I recall a dandelion waiting to burst,
an explosion, summer.

I recall the storm, its spindle of clouds.
Storm eating the sky
empty.

Your youth, my experience, lost.

I block out yesterday, the silence.
     I block out the life pressed against the windowpanes.
     The force in the room.
     The door
     a mouth gaping open.
     I block out your touch
     the resident of that body.

     This is how I mourn, wanting or not
     wandering through the day between the energy you
     transferred
     speechless.

Mund [5]

Most mornings your smile is
so wide, your furthest peaks
are revealed, pushed against an
under bite of hills. Today the storm
has closed the gaps between the sky,
a sealed mouth. I miss your crooked grin
hidden between a suture of clouds.

Beyond, bell adored sheep, graze
muted by storm cries. Somewhere, past
the front, Alps emerge, aging teeth,
their fillings new, Enzian and Edelweiss. Here,
the day frowns and below, the pouting highlands
lie helpless as the fog gobbles up the landscape
rendering the horizon toothless – proof that
some days nature doesn't want you to
read its lips.

---

5   *mouth in German*

Returning to the Highlands

Early
mountains rise
kicked back clouds

Wrinkle of sky
the pieces we were
have landed here

Scattered
seeds to soil
re-earthed

Below
toothy peaks
smiling

fixed as stars.

At the Foot of the Mountain

Wild/ daisies spread out on hills /wild/ our bodies blooming in bed /wild/ columbine tangled at my feet /wild/ how you chased me through the land /wild/ cold May wind /wild/ all those horrible things that I've said /wild/ black squirrel leaping next to me through the trees /wild/ my heart every time you arrive /wild/ the wagging of the branches /wild/ French kisses in three different languages /wild/ fortress of mountains /wild/ from you I can never hide /wild/ swimming in that clear lake /wild/ illness no one can see /wild/ all those seeds that we planted in black soil /wild/ children we've lost /wild/ altitudes we've scaled /wild/ fights that we've fought /wild/ trails through the forest /wild/ at each other's side /wild/ at the foot of the mountain.

CPSIA information can be obtained
at www.ICGtesting.com
Printed in the USA
LVHW042055291221
707460LV00003B/544

9 781951 088255